JEALOUS

Helping Children Cope With Jealousy

Written by Esther Adler

Illustrated by Shrutkirti Kaushal

www.brightawareness.com

www.westlakegavin.com

Westlake Gavin Publishers LLC
New York   Toronto   London

For Sara:

Your creativity inspires me.

E. A.

Disclaimer: The book does not provide mental health advice, diagnosis, or treatment. It is for educational use only. If you have questions or concerns about a child's mental health, please speak to a qualified mental health provider without delay.

Copyright © 2014 Westlake Gavin Publishers LLC

All rights reserved under International and Pan-American Copyright convention. No part of this publication may be reproduced, distributed, or transmitted in any form or by any means, including photocopying, recording, or other electronic or mechanical methods, without the prior written permission of the publisher, except for a brief quotation, critical review or where otherwise noted.

Westlake Gavin, Bright Awareness Publications, ColorFeeling Series, and associated logos are trademarks of Westlake Gavin Publishers LLC

Publisher's Cataloging-in-Publication data

Adler, Esther.
　Jealous : helping children cope with jealousy / by Esther Adler ; illustrated by Shrutkirti Kaushal.
　p. cm.
　ISBN 978-1-63231-003-3
　Series : ColorFeeling
　Summary : How children physically experience jealousy. Typical situations where children are prone to feel jealous. Practical approaches to help children manage jealousy.

[1. Jealous. 2. Emotions.] I. Kaushal, Shrutkirti. II. Title.

First Edition

10 9 8 7 6 5 4 3 2 1

This book belongs to:

_____

Foreword

As we learn more about what makes children thrive, we now know that the foundation of their emotional development is crucial to their overall psychological health. Some children have a strong aptitude in this area and an innate awareness of feelings that allow them to navigate their social-emotional environments well. Other children, however, experience challenges with recognizing, processing, and expressing their feelings.

For those children, simple childhood experiences can become challenging as they struggle with expressing and regulating their emotions. Whether a child gets angry if he's being ignored, sad if her goldfish dies, happy when he receives a gift, or jealous when her friends tell secrets—it is vital to help children become more aware of their emotions and the emotions of others.

Over the many years that I have spent counseling children, advising parents, and training mental health professionals about the children in their care, I have found that children who are able to recognize and express feelings have a much easier time forming friendships, navigating social situations, and managing their emotions.

This is why I was so excited when Esther showed me the ColorFeeling™ series. Finally, a set of books specifically designed to help children foster a healthy awareness of feelings in an engaging manner. Based on the quality of the material, it is evident that Esther based this series on her many years of experience working with children as a practicing licensed Mental Health Counselor.

I would like to point out a number of qualities that make this series especially useful for parents, therapists, and teachers and why I am recommending it so highly:

1. Each book in the ColorFeeling™ series associates a specific color and animal character with a feeling. Since emotions are an abstract concept, this multi-pronged approach is a cognitively clever way to help children learn to identify specific feelings.

2. The illustrations used throughout the books are magnetic, vivid, and uncluttered. They will be sure to captivate and hold the child's interest.

3. Each book focuses on just one feeling, allowing the educator to hone in on the specifics of that feeling with clarity and attention.

4. There is continuity between the books in the series. Children will delight in seeing their favorite characters and scenes reappear in other books of the series in different emotional contexts.

5. Each feeling is explored in depth and presented in a consistent manner as follows: a) common ways that children experience the physical effects of the feeling; b) typical situations where a child might be prone to experience the feeling; and c) coping skills to help the child manage the feeling.

6. To reinforce the message, there are optional interactive exercises woven throughout the book and a series of worksheets at the end.

7. Regardless of the child's knowledge about feelings or the child's coping ability, children of all ability levels can benefit from the series.

In my work as a psychologist, I look for tools that parents, teachers, and mental health professionals can use to help the children in their care. The ColorFeeling™ series has found a permanent place in my toolbox and I encourage you to utilize this resource as well.

Dr. Rona Miles, PsyD, CSP

NYS Licensed Psychologist
NYS Certified School Psychologist
Lecturer Doctoral Scholar
Brooklyn College of the City University of New York

When I feel jealous, my mouth tastes sour like a green pickle.

When I feel jealous, I can't stop thinking that I want it too.

I feel jealous when my sister has a bigger piece of cake than me.

I feel jealous when my friend has a new toy.

I feel jealous when my parents go out with my brother.

I feel jealous when people tell secrets.

Sometimes I feel jealous and I don't know why.

What makes you feel jealous?

When you feel jealous, what do you want to do?

When I feel jealous,
I can ask to share.

When I feel jealous, I can express my feelings.

When I feel jealous, I can think of all the special things that belong to me.

When you feel jealous, what could you do?

This is how I look when I feel jealous:

Glue or tape a picture of how you look when you feel jealous.

What makes you feel jealous?

1. _____

2. _____

3. _____

4. _____

This worksheet is not a diagnostic tool. It is for educational use only and should be tailored to each child's needs.
Please contact a qualified mental health provider if you have any questions or concerns about your child's mental health.
Copyright © 2014 Westlake Gavin Publishers LLC. All rights reserved.
Worksheet may be printed and copied for educational use if this copyright notice is retained.
See **www.brightawareness.com/print** for full disclaimer, terms of use, and to print additional copies.

Write a story about a time when you felt jealous.

_____

_____

_____

_____

_____

_____

Draw a picture of a time when you felt jealous.

What can you do to help a person who is jealous feel less jealous?

1. _____

2. _____

3. _____

4. _____

Circle what you could do when you feel jealous.
Cross out what you should not do when you feel jealous.

Take a friend's toy without permission	Tell someone how you feel	Ask your friend to share her toy with you
Say, "I don't care. I don't want it anyway."	Tell your brother you don't like what he has	Ask an adult to help you
Think about all the special things you have	*Write something else you could do*	*Write something else you should not do*

This worksheet is not a diagnostic tool. It is for educational use only and should be tailored to each child's needs. Please contact a qualified mental health provider if you have any questions or concerns about your child's mental health.
Copyright © 2014 Westlake Gavin Publishers LLC. All rights reserved.
Worksheet may be printed and copied for educational use if this copyright notice is retained.
See **www.brightawareness.com/print** for full disclaimer, terms of use, and to print additional copies.

About the Author

Esther Adler, LMHC, received her undergraduate degree in Psychology and graduate degree in Mental Health Counseling from Brooklyn College of the City University of New York. Esther is a New York State licensed Mental Health Counselor who provides counseling for children of all ages in schools and privately. In her work within the field, Esther saw the need for the ColorFeeling™ series to help children develop a healthy awareness of their feelings. Esther resides in New York with her husband and six children.

About the Illustrator

Shrutkirti Kaushal was born and raised in Jodhpur, India. From a young age, she was inspired to draw. She received a diploma in Commercial Art from the Board of Technical Education, Rajasthan and a diploma in Television graphics and Animation from the Asian Academy of Film and Television, Noida. Presently, Shrutkirti is a freelance artist who specializes in illustrating children's books for authors worldwide. Shrutkirti resides in Indore, India with her husband and young son who love to watch her create art.

www.brightawareness.com

- Subscribe to our email newsletter for updates and special discounts.
- Friend us on Facebook for fun contests, coupons, and lots of surprises.
- Download free printables.
- Give us feedback. We love to hear from our readers.
    - ✓ What did you like most about the book?
    - ✓ What can be improved?
    - ✓ Which title would you like to see next in this series?
- Spread the word. Post your review on Amazon.com and other sites.

Visit www.brightawareness.com for all the above and more

www.ingramcontent.com/pod-product-compliance
Lightning Source LLC
Chambersburg PA
CBHW061151070526
44584CB00034B/4485